THIS IS HOME

THIS IS HOME
JEFFREY ALAN MARKS

WITH KATHRYN O'SHEA-EVANS
FOREWORD BY JOHN SALADINO

RIZZOLI
NEW YORK

New York · Paris · London · Milan

For Gregory, James, and Sister:
Home is where you are.

My Montecito studio—with the famous rowboat that has followed me on the journey.

CONTENTS

FOREWORD

Every home should be a sanctuary. Upon entering it, you should immediately feel physically and emotionally protected. Inside, ideally there are two different but equally important kinds of spaces that metaphorically might be described as cocoons. We all need spaces that offer comfort and security, and shelter from the cold, noise, or darkness outside. But, paradoxically, we also need spaces that liberate us from terra firma, allowing our spirits to soar and our imaginations to take flight.

Jeffrey accomplishes that concept—home as sanctuary—in every space he designs. He harnesses architecture to create cathedrals and cocoons, and then imbues them with furnishings drawn from the pool of time. In that approach, his work is both English and American at once, and incorporates ideas new and old. Yet there is one overarching constant throughout: comfort.

Much of that welcoming warmth derives from the fact that Jeffrey is a true romantic with a love of period furnishings, but also a modernist in the way he abstracts the placing of objects. The resulting spaces feel serene and organic to the human eye, as naturally arranged as the trees and stones beyond our windows. It's the safe haven of nature we're so drawn to in Jeffrey's rooms, not just because of what nature is, but because we are nature. Nature is in us all.

—John Saladino

INTRODUCTION

When I wrote my first book I titled it *The Meaning of Home*, but at that point I really didn't understand what a home truly was.

When I was growing up, my family moved all over California, allowing me to experience the best of the state, from the most beautiful beaches in La Jolla, to the snowy mountains of Lake Tahoe. By the time I was an adult I was a natural vagabond, so when I had the opportunity to study in Europe after college, I found myself settling in London for design school. I fell in love with the historical weight and permanence of the architecture during my seven years there. As much as I loved England, though, my deep California roots eventually got the better of me, and I moved back to start my design career. Working my way up the coast from La Jolla to Hollywood to Santa Monica, I met new friends, partners, and clients. I was so invested in how my clients lived—where they liked their favorite coffee mugs placed or how they preferred their towels folded—that I felt like I was a true expert in all things home. The irony was, with the exception of sharing a home with my dogs, I never felt truly settled.

Then my life changed. I met my now husband, fell in love, and got married. Two years later we welcomed our life force daughter, James, into the world. Informed by our prescribed notions of what a home should be and what a childhood should look like, we started on our one-and-a-half-year journey to find our place, considering everywhere from Austin to Aspen. Throughout our exploration we stumbled on new projects that inspired me: breathtaking private islands and luxurious compounds; working with friends on their forever home on Lake Austin; and with new friends designing their next chapter in

Newport Beach. When it came to our family, though, we kept designing and redesigning our life. In 2018, we purchased a beach house in Montecito, and we spent the next nine months moving from rental house to rental house while we waited for permits. James transitioned from a swaddled, bug-eyed baby to a toddler taking her first steps in a friend's pool house in Sonoma. Life had become a chaotic but exhilarating adventure.

Once our Montecito house was done, however, we felt we were on the beach too much. We were running out of sunscreen, metaphorically speaking. After spending seven years in California, my husband was eager to reunite with his family on the East Coast. With James in tow, we tackled updating a historic East Hampton home on his family's property for summers to come. The changes in our lives kept my mind running as I became more and more inspired to design and sketch new collections and projects for myself. The work I did for my clients also became a way to test products and crafts that I had seen on all our travels.

As kids do, James continued to mature and grow. Her needs shifted and expanded. I didn't want her to grow up the way I had—being moved around often—but I realized that we had been nomads since the day she was born. We are a family who love change and beauty, and our houses had become skins that we could easily shed in order to grow into new ones. Change is good, but for us it was time to find a place where we could put down roots—a place where we could be closer to Gregory's family, and where the schools are some of the best in the nation. When our new house in Greenwich, Connecticut, fell into our laps, it just felt like the right place.

Now, having lived all over the world, I have realized that my true meaning of home is the memories you create in that house—no matter where it is. I now understand that we love

our rooms not because of the dramatic de Gournay wallpaper or the picture-ready Plain English kitchens, but because of the people we bring with us over the threshold and the experiences we share with them, from holiday celebrations to building fires in the living room to impromptu dinners around the kitchen island. Homes are meant to be lived in.

I think we weren't all meant to live in the same house for generations, the way our ancestors did. Change, while often scary, is where greatness happens. And I believe that a home is the nucleus of it all. Life is all about embracing change and finding your next adventure, whether it be in your current neighborhood or somewhere across the world.

As a designer, I look back on the last thirty years as a book with many chapters, each filled with characters and adventures that informed my style and career. For now, my story continues within these one-hundred--year-old stone walls—with my main character, James, guiding me to my next plot twist. I'll see you on the journey ahead.

BUTTERFLY BEACH

They say that when you meet the person who will become your future spouse, you "just know." Having spent more than three decades as an interior designer, I can't help but feel that way about real estate.

Years ago, when I first encountered the 1925 Montecito house that would eventually become our family's first home together, I was enamored to the core. The exterior massing reminded me of the houses dotting the English countryside, with its storybook architecture surrounded by sprawling lush green lawns.

So six years ago when my husband, Gregory, and I spotted a for sale placard posted out front when we were on our way to Marin one morning, we took it as a sign. We would be welcoming our beautiful daughter, James, in six months, and we'd been contemplating decamping from Los Angeles for our other home close to Gregory's family in East Hampton. But I was a bit reluctant to leave LA, and finding this place put a pause on our plans. What better entrée to the world could James have than a cozy California cottage, where she could easily roam unfettered under the oak trees and pines?

There was just one complication: the house needed some love, and fast. Over the decades it had been subject to an array of bad renovations, with cramped ceilings and dated finishes! I longed to create a tailored home with maximum luxury within a comparatively simple cottage backdrop.

So I did what I love to do: I rolled up my chambray sleeves and got to work. In nine months, I basically brought it down to the studs, gutting the entire kitchen. Then I raised a lot of the low ceilings, added radiant underfloor heating, built a guesthouse, and redid the garden. I am always deeply invested in the architecture of my projects, and I put on my hard hat to take over the building site and get it all done before our baby arrived.

I wanted the freshly renovated interiors to feel like they had always been there; that's one key to the British cottage look I love. My design DNA was forever changed after I was discovered by a modeling scout at a café in Sloane Square, London. I used the money from my modeling contract to pay for London's Inchbald School of Design. Spending weekdays roaming the streets of London and weekends traveling to Milan or Paris for shoots, I received a full education in European style. Through guest talks at school, I was introduced to and able to work in small ways for British tastemakers David Hicks, Nicky Haslam, John Stefanidis, and the Colefax and Fowler gang. These experiences were my real education in interior design: their rooms look as if they had evolved over generations. There was so much to see! I'd noticed my most stylish friends would add the simplest thing next to the most outrageously glamorous aesthetic choice—and it would somehow make it all appear plain, simple, and delightfully unpretentious.

In our Montecito living room, layered rugs and a custom red light fixture from Urban Electric add to the collected effect. The 1920s box covered with shells on the coffee table is from Lee Stanton Antiques; we tuck candles inside the box when they are not in use. The sofa is from my own collection for A. Rudin.

My husband and I have always felt close to the sea, so we wanted to be surrounded by playful nods to nautical style, such as manila fiber ropes acting as banisters up the stairs or the old Abercrombie & Fitch rowboat that is suspended from the ceiling over my desk. We employed English and American antiques we'd collected on the East Coast in an effort to feel like we do during our blissful East Coast summers year-round. That layer of history makes our home feel more like East Hampton than a typical California beach house.

Elements of texture are essential for making a recently redone house feel historic. I'll often ask painters to apply four or five coats to get the depth and brushstrokes that only old-fashioned natural bristle brushes—never rollers—can provide. I'm not a big lover of drywall,

ABOVE: We used a casual rope in place of balusters to give a more nautical look. OPPOSITE: The Lindsey Adelman light fixture references sea glass floats. FOLLOWING PAGES: I designed a custom sectional through Howe London for our sunroom; the chair in the foreground is a Gustavian antique. Window treatments are made with fabric from LA's own Otis Textiles; the lamp was fashioned from a circa 1900s rototiller.

so we added shiplap to any wall that was bare. I needed that texture to visually unite the home's many disparate spaces. Where shiplap wouldn't work, I used wall upholstery and grass cloth to add solidity and make our little jewel box come together. To that end, in our primary bedroom—which we reconfigured so the mullioned windows would face the Santa Ynez mountains and thick stands of pine trees—I paper-backed an indigo linen wallcovering that reminds me of vintage denim. It is cocooning, just like your favorite pair of jeans.

So much of the house is nostalgic and references our past as well as our future, like the antiques we've brought home from favorite trips and places we'll take our family again. In

PREVIOUS PAGES: I designed the custom zinc-wrapped hood in our Montecito kitchen. The leather handles on the island and custom verdigris light fixture add texture. The high gloss ceiling reads like a mirror; its reflective quality enlarges the space. ABOVE: I had the interior of our Plain English kitchen cabinets painted the same blue as the mudroom to serve as a punctuation point behind custom mesh inserts. OPPOSITE: Under the stairs, we tucked a dog nook for our beloved late lab, Coal. The Jacques Adnet wrapped leather coatrack was a Paris flea market find. FOLLOWING PAGES: The sunny kitchen window nook features a wraparound banquette.

PREVIOUS PAGES: Bar cabinets are often a wonderful place to tuck a painting or two; you can take in the art while shaking your drink. ABOVE: De Gournay wallpaper and an old banker's light from Switzerland bring charm into the powder room. The mirror is from my collection for Palecek. OPPOSITE: I brought the standing seam ceiling of our roof into the mudroom so it would feel like an outside space. The antique paver limestones are from Exquisite Surfaces; behind the cabinetry, we've hidden two washers and a dryer. FOLLOWING PAGES: I transformed an old storage shed into our pool house, with a built-in banquette upholstered in an indoor/outdoor fabric I designed for Kravet.

PREVIOUS PAGES: In our primary bedroom, I upholstered the walls in a Rose Tarlow denim-like linen.
ABOVE: When we're in Montecito, we love to pile into this window nook and read with James; I
used my Kravet fabric collection for the throw pillows and upholstery. OPPOSITE: We custom-made
this double vanity—a feature in my last two houses, where I turned extra bedrooms into primary
bathrooms—so Gregory and I can talk while we're prepping for the day.

ABOVE: The vanity in this guest bathroom is custom; the wallpaper is Phillip Jeffries. OPPOSITE: I painted the exposed beams and ceiling in this guest room Farrow & Ball's Dimpse in high gloss, which helps the small space feel more expansive. FOLLOWING PAGES: For James's playroom—which also serves as an extra guest room—I designed a space-saving built-in bed.

the sunlit playroom of our daughter, James, we opted to upholster the walls. We mixed some

pink into the paint for the ceiling above, so it practically glows.

One of the spaces I reworked most thoroughly was our kitchen. Inspired by my love of

English houses, I wanted it to call to mind the "below the stairs" cook spaces and sculleries

found in old manor houses. I juxtaposed a clean-lined zinc range hood with needed rusticity;

a French stove; and a fixture over the lengthy thirteen-foot island that lends the room

dimension and history. It also supplies a warm, welcoming light under which James and I

got our cardio in by running around that island giggling a thousand times! To bring the

outdoors inside, we painted the cabinet interiors sky blue. We didn't have a formal dining

ABOVE: The fabric on the walls of James's playroom is from Colefax and Fowler, and it was one of the first patterns I fell in love with in design school. The chair is an English antique from the early 1900s. OPPOSITE: I love a welcoming corner banquette. The mirror and table are from my collection for Palecek; the carpet is by The Rug Company.

room, so we'd eat in the kitchen nook, which we loved for its wraparound banquette and the sun that streamed in on three sides. Or we'd light hurricane candles on the patio and dine outside by the stone fireplace. In the pink glow of twilight, James would flit around the grounds like the happiest little hummingbird.

In the end this house was everything that Gregory and I could have wanted for James's first home, and it became an indelible backdrop for some of my best memories—with these humans that I adore. We especially loved our walks to Butterfly Beach for sunset cocktails— and James practically grew up before our eyes there, right on the shore.

ABOVE: Our daughter, James, age three, in a fanciful flurry of bubbles. OPPOSITE: In James's room, we placed a Gustavian bed from Galerie Half. The jungle-cat wallpaper is Hermès, and the blanket was custom made for us by Malibu Market & Design. The papier-mâché animal mounts are from Nickey Kehoe.

ABOVE: The Dutch door on our guesthouse is painted in Narrows from Portola Paints in high gloss; I found the metal lampshade above it in Amsterdam, and designed the armature to place it on the house with Paul Ferrante. OPPOSITE: My home office in Montecito. FOLLOWING PAGES: Our exterior patio, where we dined much of the time. The bench is an old English antique that we re-covered. The limestone-topped table is by David Sutherland; Palecek's Dockside chairs are handwoven with marine-grade rope.

THE
WEDGE

Dorothy was right: there's no place like home.
So when my wonderful friends—parents of three who spend the majority of the year at their town house in London—had the opportunity to revamp their waterfront house in the same Southern California beach town where they both grew up, they jumped—and high. Their home sits on this magical point on a peninsula where a misty bay meets the ocean, and you can hop in and out of a Duffy boat at your leisure. However, the house had been built in the early 1990s and wasn't living up to its locale. They'd been keeping it as a rental, and tenants left it looking like a nineteenth-century New Orleans bordello: wine-red walls, dark wood trim, flashy light fixtures, and heavy window coverings. If you didn't know better, you would have thought you'd wandered into a 10,000-square-foot wine room, circa 1982.

Still, the property had plenty going for it—including an oceanfront perch on three generous lots that provide expansive, lush grounds. Our goal from the start was to mix my friends' love of English style with their deep California roots. We also added

a smattering of a Saint-Tropez vibe for good, glamorous measure, as this family spends time on the Côte d'Azur every summer. They loved my own home in Santa Monica Canyon for which I had done the architecture, interiors, and grounds. For that reason, they didn't hire an architect or landscape architect. I devised all the structural tweaks to the fenestration and interiors myself—gutting the house inside and out in just a year with the help of my favorite local builder, Jake Winkle, who tells me he loves that the resulting home "embraces coastal living, with large expansive decks and vantage points from every room."

Arguably the biggest issue in the original home was that the primary bedroom was the darkest room in the house, with hardly any windows looking out to the water. Talk about a missed opportunity! I opened it all up, and added French doors that exit onto a new wraparound terrace overlooking the Pacific. You feel like you can almost touch the boats as they whir in and out of the harbor.

Like a strong wave reshaping a sandy shoreline, we excised most of the downstairs and bedroom suites to start entirely fresh.

We even got rid of the sweeping entry staircase. Instead, we installed a comparatively streamlined *escalier* that we arranged specifically so you can see the boats bobbing at sea when you walk up the risers. It was also important to me to beadboard many of the walls with tongue and groove, which I have in many of

PAGES 52–53: A pottery lamp by Dumais Made illuminates the living room, with sofas by Howe London. PREVIOUS PAGES: We had the custom marble table made in Italy; the leather-wrapped lamp is Jacques Adnet. We painted the floors Farrow & Ball's Light Blue. OPPOSITE: To retain the airiness in the dining room, I custom designed this table with a black cut oak top and metal base. The lacquered bench is by Sawkille Co. (from March in San Francisco), painted in Farrow & Ball's Inchyra Blue. The vintage stone stools from Blackman Cruz add texture.

ABOVE: The stair rail is painted a custom jean blue that echoes the sea. Anchoring the hallway: a metal desk from 1920s Britain. OPPOSITE: We sheathed the ceiling of the TV room in grass cloth to up the cozy factor. I repurposed the doorway beams from another part of the house after stripping and bleaching them, and added shiplap to the walls for texture. The antique leather lounge chairs, designed in 1964 by Angelo Mangiarotti, are from Blackman Cruz.

PREVIOUS PAGES: For a warehouse-style kitchen, I installed decorative industrial windows and built two islands to transform the large room into a workhorse. The pair of Havana pendant lights with leather chains are by Ralph Pucci. OPPOSITE AND ABOVE: Middleton Pink from Farrow & Ball creates a dreamy backdrop for flower arranging in the laundry room, especially juxtaposed against the petite integrated granite sink.

my own homes. It makes the rooms a note lighter, a note happier—not so serious! The ceilings here are so high that they qualify as cavernous, and adding this textural cladding imbued the interior with a touch of cottage style, warming it up instantly.

Actually, this whole house project was largely an exercise in adding jolts of color, but not in a cloying way. We installed white oak floors, topping them with a few simple woven cotton and light wool rugs that put people at ease as they come in barefoot from the dock or beach. Where we kept some of the existing wide-plank pine, we painted it a greeny blue, watery color. (The harbor outside is not always blue: it changes in the light, and

ABOVE: We sheathed the entire pool bathroom in Moroccan tile from Exquisite Surfaces. The blue glass mirror is vintage and lends a nautical note. OPPOSITE: This window seat was inspired by one in my Montecito home; it overlooks the water so you can watch the yachts bob. The sheepskin chair is from Galerie Half; the throw pillows are in fabric by Christopher Farr Cloth. I found the accordion light at an antiques fair in England.

OPPOSITE: The custom Richard Wrightman bed is upholstered in a Zak+Fox fabric. The bench at the foot of the bed is a Swedish antique, which brings in the aura of history. ABOVE: The Lucca Antiques bench in the primary room's closet inspired the entire scheme for the simple cabinetry, complete with Richard Wrightman leather straps in lieu of metal drawer pulls.

ABOVE AND OPPOSITE: We gutted this primary bathroom space and the adjacent closet; sometimes starting from scratch is the best way to go. Fish swirling on the custom de Gournay wallpaper are a perfect fit in a room overlooking the water.

sometimes skews deep forest green.) With the high gloss paint, you almost feel like you're walking on water, and here, at the edge of the sea, you very nearly are.

Together, my clients and I scoured the countryside beyond London looking for pieces that were thoroughly staid and British, yet would also feel relaxed in the California light. I also took a whirl through each of their homes to select a few works in their existing art collection to bring here, lending the house an authentic sensibility that would reflect their travels and varying interests. It's quite balanced, with everything from modern photography to cheekier pieces.

In the kitchen, I talked them into keeping some of the brickwork. They were a little nervous about it because they loathed the original kitchen's red brick so much, but I knew that when painted white it would be very architectural, lending the feel of an industrial warehouse in London. The trick was balancing it by opening up all the walls around the kitchen, so I blew out all the pantries and closets (as devotees of fresh fruits and vegetables, they didn't need so much dry storage) to allow the kitchen to be one big room at the center of the home. Around it, we hung steel casement windows that allow you to peer into the adjacent living room while still making the kitchen the confined core of the house.

Throughout, you'll find surfaces that are burnished by time—leather, wood, marble—which is part of their beauty. In a few years, each tea spot and wine ring will be less of a blot, and more of a memory.

This magnolia tree was dying when we began the renovation, but we spent months nursing it back to health and I'm so glad we did. The shape of these fiberglass Positano chairs from Ralph Pucci reflects the billowing sails just beyond.

SULLIVAN CANYON

Los Angeles is clearly no stranger to a rock star aesthetic. But a house with a rock star aesthetic on a two-acre working horse farm within the thumping heart of LA? Any movie producer would agree that that is cinematic.

This particular couple—a major music executive and an equestrian who travels the world with her horses—found me by watching my show on Bravo. I'll never forget what she said when she first called: "I love your character. I think you're hilarious! I think you'd be fun to build a house with." There was a bit of a hiccup, though. While she absolutely loved me, she hated pretty much every design choice that I love. She didn't want anything with a California feel. Absolutely no window coverings, and she instantly nixed any blues! "Nope, I don't want it!" But we clicked personally, and she trusted me to make her vision happen.

We took over the architecture plans for the newly built home from Backen & Backen, a firm in St. Helena, California, and set about making the structure and spaces a bit quirkier and more fun, to her exacting taste. The original proposal arranged a U-shaped house around a pool; now, it would embrace gardens. She longed to pick out vintage sinks and wanted the home's high ceilings sheathed in corrugated metal and its floors made of poured concrete for an industrial gallery feel. We sourced finds together by shopping flea markets everywhere from upstate New York to Europe, while she often eschewed my regular antiquarian haunts for being too fussy. And what we brought home—the worn sign we transformed into a rolling barn door; the hulking factory table that was perfect for the outdoor kitchen—fit her original rock star fantasy perfectly. Like the composer who can instantly strike the right note, she zeroed in on what she wanted. Much of what you see here was custom made for her, down to the four-poster bed that was handcrafted by a woodworker in Venice Beach. I'll never forget her coming back from a trip to France and tossing a zebra hide on my desk—very Miranda Priestly from *The Devil Wears Prada*, in the best possible way—and giving me my marching orders: "Deal with this. Make it something fun!" (It's now a streamlined ottoman.)

PAGES 74–75: The landscape design is by GSLA Studio. PAGE 76: The side table is a reproduction of an Italian antique from Caché, in West Hollywood. PAGE 77: The overhead fixture is a custom beaded piece from Paul Ferrante. OPPOSITE: I designed the two built-in benches that flank the fireplace and had them made with poured concrete. The stools are from Galerie Half.

This family all love to gather in one space where the kids can do homework while the parents read and poke around on their laptops, so we created an English-style library arranged around a worktable I designed. She wanted all the chairs to be piggly-wiggly and different, which adds a comforting, homey feeling to the otherwise industrial room. Her chosen red, rusty tones warm up the chilly envelope of the architecture.

She pushed the design, clearly, but there were plenty of times when I pushed her, too. The chandelier in the living room is one example: she brought back from Paris an inspirational photo of a light fixture she wanted to use, but it felt a little banal to me. "No, you can't have that," I said. "I'll make you a better one!" So I commissioned one of my go-to lighting designers to create a piece that is dripping with tiny metal beads. It's very romantic and playful, yet still industrial enough to suit her tastes.

The original plans for a pool were scratched to house nine horses comfortably on their two-acre property; she wanted to be able to see them from their living areas. We swapped the pool for a picking garden that I painstakingly designed with landscape architecture firm GSLA Studio. Now, the family can putter out and grab the freshest possible lettuce, kale, and herbs to take to their outdoor kitchen. It's part Joni Mitchell, part Led Zeppelin. The horses have it made.

PAGES 80–81: A pair of leather love seats and ironwood tables from JF Chen suit the home's rock 'n' roll vibe. PREVIOUS PAGES: Adjacent to the horse stables, rows of *tuteurs* await climbing vines in the vegetable garden. OPPOSITE: Just off the herb garden I tucked an outdoor kitchen with reclaimed barnwood walls for texture.

PAGE 86: We transformed a vintage sign we found in an old Hollywood prop house into a sliding barn door leading into the wine room. PAGE 87: A 1960s artichoke pendant lamp juxtaposes beautifully with the Texas barn siding ceiling in the library. ABOVE: A nineteenth-century English rocking chair and lengthy side table bring storied appeal to the primary bedroom. OPPOSITE: The magic is in the mix, such as this Italian giltwood settee and clean-lined canopy bed.

OPPOSITE: An antique Italian shell bed anchors a daughter's room; it was inherited from her grandfather in Europe. ABOVE: Custom wallcovering by Nathalie Lété and a tufted chair upholstered in California's iconic state flag.

THE STRAND

On the shores of Manhattan Beach, my clients sought to re-create the sprawling residential landscapes of Montecito— olive trees, pea-gravel paths, and rolling hills that appear to go on forever against an expanse of blue sea—on a smaller scale.

It helped that they purchased the lot next door to their existing beach cottage when it became available, creating a tidy one-acre compound that linked the land between two streets on the block. Once we knocked down their original home, we

could go all-in on their dream house. They'd enlisted a longtime friend of mine, Grant C. Kirkpatrick of KAA Design Group in Los Angeles, to design the structure, and I came aboard before they broke ground—bringing my own toolbox of architectural magic tricks for some finessing of the plans.

To start, I convinced them to swap the guesthouse they'd planned out back for a pool pavilion.
In their new 8,000-square-foot primary house, this family of three wouldn't really need separate guest quarters, but a pool house where they could host their son's friends was key (when you have a teenager, creating a hangout spot where they'll actually *want* to be with their crew is vital). We kept the Montecito vernacular top of mind when designing the landscape, with its graceful olive trees, leafy hedges that serve to obscure neighboring houses, and an expanse of green lawn that unfurls with a natural edge along the pool.

Inside the home, limiting the color palette to the region's seaside tones—including sands, surf blues, and the inky blacks of the night sky—helped to expand the spaces visually. I also sought to add a snug, almost English-inspired sensibility to Kirkpatrick's uncluttered modern architecture. I sensed that the clients leaned more traditional Hamptons style than modernist in all their picks, and the home needed some layering and cozying up. In the dining space that overlooks the pool, we created a built-in

OPPOSITE: A vintage English chair from LA's own Obsolete brings texture to a newly built home; the lamp is by Rose Uniacke. I designed the side table myself; the top is wrapped in leather for a soft effect. The latticework wall—designed by the architect, Grant C. Kirkpatrick—extends from the lower level to the top floor and serves as a screen. FOLLOWING PAGES: An old Swedish armoire from Lief Gallery in Los Angeles kicked off the color palette in the great room, where the fireplace is clad in iron. A circa 1910 art stand from Galerie Half acts as a pedestal for pottery.

ABOVE: We enlisted the help of Hub of the House Studio in West Hollywood to help organize these clients' fabulous tableware and kitchen accessories, transforming the wet bar into a full floor-to-ceiling showpiece pantry that houses all their goodies. OPPOSITE: When we constructed the house, we poured concrete around this bench and the steel-case windows were built around it before the flooring was laid. The table is by John Saladino.

bench that appears to levitate over the floor (it's actually attached to the steel windows by prongs), made plush and welcoming with a thick custom cushion. I wanted it to be part of the floor-to-ceiling window yet also disappear to keep the view paramount. Across the table, an antique ladderback chair I hauled over from England balances all the streamlined modernity with a whisper to the past.

I echoed those steel-case windows from the dining nook in the sitting room, where we sheathed part of the wall in black steel, then softened it up with a beadboard ceiling and our furniture choices, including a John Saladino sofa that is one of my favorites (and not just because he was one of the first decorators I met when I was in my twenties, and I've always admired him so much). The green-aqua horizontal stripe on that sofa sets the tone in the space, where soft yet modern lines prevail. Above one end of the sofa, we hung a library wall sconce from Soane, one of my go-to stores in London.

Throughout the home, I employed antique rugs underfoot. Because the architecture was so airy and light feeling, we needed the rugs to anchor the rooms and give them stability.

Sometimes, you don't want the quintessential California beach house—you want something a little more solid and timeworn. It's that mix of modern and more storied touches that will make an interior age well for generations to come. This home is proof that, whether in Manhattan Beach or East Hampton, house size doesn't matter—style does.

OPPOSITE: I echoed the grid of the window formation in the adjacent steel wall, which can slide over the glass for privacy. The Cape sofa is by John Saladino, upholstered in a Manuel Canovas fabric. FOLLOWING PAGES: The outdoor bar overlooks the beach on one side, and the pool on the other. This tile backsplash inspired my new collection for The Tile Shop.

ABOVE: A stone wall gives the pool an aura of history. OPPOSITE: West Hollywood's Hub of the House Studio helped me design the kitchen, with cabinets by Plain English. I brought in some playfulness by adding a geometric pattern to the Richard Wrightman chairs, to keep the room from reading as too neutral.

PREVIOUS PAGES: The family collects in this club room, with George Smith seating and a custom table I designed, for a tradition of Wednesday night dinners. ABOVE: With floral curtains and a cozy window seat, her study is a bit more feminine than the rest of the house. OPPOSITE: We brought a lot of finishes and fabrics into the primary bathroom, including the antiqued mirror on the wall at left that reflects the adjacent beach. I love the formality of the window treatments here; I'd rather have three times the width or no curtains at all. FOLLOWING PAGES: The primary bedroom has a seating area surrounding a firepit just beyond its doors: indoor/outdoor living at its best.

SUMMER TRAIL

This fabulous client and I had a definite "meet cute." We first started talking while dancing next to each other in a class at Tracy Anderson! She is a former film producer who is now a world-class polo player with homes and horse farms all over the world, from Mexico to Santa Barbara. At the time, she was designing a personal dance studio and asked me to come help. It was only the start of our fun projects together—fitting, given the way we met.

OPPOSITE: We laid a checkerboard floor from Exquisite Surfaces in this Aspen foyer to add a certain formality; it also bolsters the classical effect of the Venetian plaster walls. A duo of bronze benches flank a custom round table of my own design.
ABOVE: An eighteenth-century Gustavian secretary from Galerie Half.

For her family's longtime property outside Aspen, which was originally built in 1910, she longed to create a simple retreat that would be a serene, airy foil for her art collection. The existing structure had the brick massing of a Normandy cottage, and interior rooms were very poky. So we opened up the architecture, restructuring much of it to suit the free-range way that families live today. We gutted the interior and added on some 2,000 square feet, plus a pool and pool house. Nodding to the storied estates of Europe, we created an open reception hall on the site where the original kitchen stood, complete with a faded limestone checkerboard floor underfoot. We also devised a way to include both a family wing and a separate wing for guests—a sanity-saving measure, as anyone who has hosted visitors for an extended length of time can attest!

Adding to the rustic Europe-in-Colorado feel are Venetian plaster walls, which we employed in all the common areas for texture and a warming effect in rooms with soaring ceilings. You won't see many antiques; she is just not an antiques person. Still, to me antiques add so much that can be hard to achieve with new furniture, so I included one eighteenth-century Swedish sideboard

The tête-à-tête in the great room is my own design for A. Rudin; the rug is a grid of banded hair-on-hide from Austin, Texas—based Kyle Bunting.

in the entry. I loved juxtaposing unusual pieces throughout with her carefully curated art, such as a tête-à-tête that I designed for A. Rudin that sits under a large-scale photograph by Drew Doggett of horses stampeding across the snow.

One of my favorite rooms in this home is the breakfast room, which is in the oldest part of the original house. Previously, it was a sunroom that straddled a bedroom, but now it sits beside the kitchen. I think it's the perfect place for sipping your morning caffeine jolt of choice as the light streams over the snowcaps and in through the arched windows. Making it especially welcoming are the radiant heated floors: when it snows, you can sit there and take it all in from the coziest, warmest perch imaginable. In this space, the client really wanted to feel like she was in the snow—one with it, as it swirled around in thick, downy flakes. By leaving the windows bare, that was achieved.

The client and I still remain good friends, and now I get to watch her on her own private polo field near one of her other homes in Summerland, California, winning every time!

My mirror for Palecek brings added light to the dining room, where the walls and ceiling are plaster. The table and chair upholstery are by Rose Tarlow, while the chairs themselves are from my collection for A. Rudin.

ABOVE: A pool becomes a de facto private swimming hole at a mountain house. OPPOSITE: We selected the Urban Electric overhead fixtures in the sunroom because they mirror the shapes of the architecture. FOLLOWING PAGES: Indoor/outdoor views of the breakfast room, which is in the original part of the home. The room's design is anchored by a Richard Wrightman table. Heated slate floors underfoot eliminate the need for a rug.

ABOVE: We installed a thicker island countertop than is standard, at three inches. I also painted the base a different hue from the cabinets; I wanted the island itself to feel different from the rest of the kitchen, so it would look more like a piece of furniture than a built-in. OPPOSITE: The counter stools in stained and oiled white oak are Richard Wrightman; floors are Exquisite Surfaces. FOLLOWING PAGES: In the primary bedroom, the David Sutherland Bonsai table was made of concrete and steel and brings a note of poetry to the corner.

BAKER'S BAY

This hush-hush 585-acre island is as idyllic as a Caribbean retreat gets, with powdery white sand beaches and clear-as-glass turquoise seas stretching infinitely toward the horizon. Because it's members only, it's long been a retreat for boldface names and glitterati.

Adding to the serene charm is the fact that there are no cars, only golf carts to whir around the Tom Fazio–designed golf course and winding trails. Talk about a golfer's paradise! I felt that such a blissful landscape demanded a level of custom furniture and finishes worthy of the destination, and happily, this couple agreed.

We met years ago after they toured a project of mine in Colorado, instantly fell in love with my style, and hired me for another of their homes. They're an

incredibly lovely duo, and we became fast friends. After finishing their last project, we couldn't quite say goodbye, so we jumped on their plane to the Bahamas to start our next revamp.

The goal here was a true vacation home: a relaxed, dreamy, and happy place to return to after a barefoot round of golf at sunset.

Thankfully, their chosen getaway had a clean building envelope and an expansive 13,000-square-foot floor plan with seven full suites looking out to the water. This was not the traditional Bahamian clapboard and tin-roofed cottage, to our benefit. Its minimalist lines encouraged design, drama, and romance at every turn, because they put the focus on the landscape and beaches beyond.

The place epitomizes indoor/outdoor living, with doors flung open to the island air nearly 24-7, so I knew that everything in the house would need to stand up to a salty breeze. We used linen wallpaper coated for humid air to add texture to blasé drywall, while performance fabrics allow kids and adults alike to run into the house with damp suits and sand between their toes without care. Casual, breezy living was key. After all, this is the type of place where people are happy to shed stiff city shoes in exchange for custom monogrammed flip-flops (which we ordered for guests of the house). Days are spent golfing, swimming, and stopping in at a series of tequila shacks and delightful candy huts for a sugar fix.

This entrance hall—which overlooks the sea on one side and a golf course on the other—felt cavernous, so I placed a round table in the center as a strong foundation. The rope stools are my own design for Palecek. I curtained much of the house to lend warmth.

ABOVE: I love the linear wallpaper we hung in the entrance hall behind a console of my own design. The fabric of the curtains, Cowtan & Tout's Captiva in Ocean, was my starting point for the whole house. OPPOSITE: Incorporating wingback chairs can bring a welcome note of English formality to a house—something that's especially needed in easy, breezy coastal homes.

I found it challenging to establish a layered feeling without using antiques, which this couple determined would be a note too serious for their vacationland getaway.

The trick was to add theater in other ways, through lighting and bespoke details, such as the clamshell light fixture we found in London that now presides over the entrance hall. It became our seaworthy starting point for the entire project. One place I splurged was on the drapery: I wanted to create a cocoon. I don't usually employ printed drapery, but in this instance it was the perfect way to add a touch of playfulness that would set a very different tone from this family's more buttoned-up homes elsewhere.

Many people are afraid of using too much color, but here the family embraced it, which helped produce a jovial feeling. I wanted the house to be anchored and a little traditional—not too airy fairy—which is why I went for dark hues on some cabinet finishes and furniture in contrast to almost acidic, minty colors. The color palette of watery blues and teal greens also cooled down the travertine floors. Their sandy hue didn't exactly thrill me, but I couldn't change them, so I covered them with rugs that I had made in Guatemala with hard-wearing acrylic fabric woven throughout the soft wool and sisal natural fibers.

One of the biggest transformations was the home bar. When we first stepped foot in this room, it was so dark and brown that it looked like a watering hole for Silicon Valley techies. It had no sense of place. In both architecture and design, you

In the original kitchen, the dark brown cabinets didn't suit the scene. I painted the cabinets this bright blue to give the cooking space more of a Caribbean feel, and we hung garden lanterns to match. The barstools are my own, for Palecek.

have to remember where you are always. So I thought, OK, we're going to make this exuberant—the type of place where you can picture Bunny Mellon sipping an evening daiquiri. To give it a historic Caribbean feel, we paneled the underbelly of the bar's island for detail, and painted it and the built-in bar a soft Ibiza blue. A pair of teal scalloped pendant lights and Soane woven barstools add a dose of happiness, while a blown-up surf photograph by my Malibu-based friend Steven Lippman supplies needed muscularity to the room. Look closely, and you'll spy two flat-screen TVs hidden among the upper shelving. Like the whole house now, it's practical, but with a Palm Beach twist.

OPPOSITE: In England I found handmade Soane rattan barstools that serve as a nice punctuation point to the bar located just off the media room; the color is custom, by Soane. ABOVE: We matched the scallop on the shades of the pendant lights to Soane's Messel Green. FOLLOWING PAGES: The clients' son's favorite color is green, so we mixed a few different verdant shades in his bedroom. Green is one of the few colors you can do that with.

ABOVE: My clients let me play around with bold colors in their primary suite, which was a fun exercise. OPPOSITE: The blue lacquer-topped side table—one of a pair—is very playful; we found the pedestal topped by shells in the home's subterranean floor after a hurricane, and it's a nice conversation piece. FOLLOWING PAGES: The coral-colored mirror above the bed provides a nice pop of color in the blue Caribbean room. The carved wooden armchair is Dennis & Leen.

DOG
BEACH

I grew up in La Jolla, California, and started my once-fledgling design business on its verdant shores. So when the opportunity arose to design a contemporary Mediterranean home nearby, it felt like a homecoming of sorts—especially as the structure was being designed from the ground up by Island Architects, former neighbors of my first brick-and-mortar design headquarters.

Block by block, Coronado is one of the most charming islands in the United States, with its fanciful Victorians and the iconic Hotel Del, a red-turreted grand dame built circa 1888 and featured in the classic film *Some Like It Hot*. While my

clients love the island's history, they had a different vision for their home—one that was as clean as the horizon line on the Pacific Ocean, and in total contrast to the quaintness of the island itself. With their children now away at college, this modernist glass-walled respite was their dream vernacular and one they could design entirely for themselves.

Early on, I enlisted Los Angeles landscape architect Scott Shrader to transform the beachfront lot into a lush, private retreat that speaks in the same language as the region's topography. They call him No Grass Scott for a reason: he didn't use lawns long before that was a fashion! Shrader helped create a very fluid, indoor/outdoor experience in the home, where a flurry of succulents burst like garden roses atop the living room's graphic custom iron coffee table, and a rampart of hedges generates an ensconcing feel (not to mention a delightful wall of green that instantly soothes the soul in all seasons).

Inside, I knew there couldn't be a lot of ornament in a home that's this streamlined.

My vision was a 1940s ocean liner: classic, yet eternally modern. We maximized singular moments. In the entry hall, we built an art piece by Adam Belt that's made of mirrors and LED lights into the plaster wall; in the living room, an abstract sea turtle–patterned rug, soft as powdery sand, juxtaposes with the more formidable Swedish antiques we found on a buying trip in Europe.

OPPOSITE: We set up a bar atop a lacquered table just off the kitchen. Above it, pieces from Holly Hunt arranged in a grid feel like glass—albeit in very subtly gradient pigments of color—on the pine walls. FOLLOWING PAGES: I enlisted landscape architect Scott Shrader to assist with the naturalistic plantings, because the house is so fluid from the indoors out.

Throughout, textural additions, like the timeworn woven rocking chair from the clients' Sonoma house that we placed on a landing, add needed rusticity. These touches are wonderfully playful, and necessary; we didn't want the house to be too sparse. I was a stickler about one thing: I didn't want to see any drywall in the house. Instead, in the kitchen and entrance hall we sheathed the walls in white oak, a modern take on an English pine-paneled library, and in most of the other rooms we used earthy plaster that evokes the texture of the beach itself.

We designed the stairway—which curves like a spiraling conch shell through all four floors—to serve as an architectural mass in the middle of the house. But when our first cladding on it, steel, felt too chilly, we ended up finishing it in dark gray plaster. With a stair runner rug trimmed in cobalt blue, each step brings you back to the sea just outside the door.

OPPOSITE: You'll find pieces by Richard Wrightman—who designed this handcrafted table and leather benches—in any house that I do. The articulated light fixture overhead supplies a lightness; the art piece by Mel Bochner suits these homeowners, who are always laughing.
FOLLOWING PAGES: I custom designed the asymmetrical coffee table, a beautiful juxtaposition on the hand-knotted silk rug by Christopher Farr. The sculpture in the garden is from the 1930s.

PREVIOUS PAGES: An art deco painting from France presides over the steel fireplace, designed by La Jolla's Island Architects. THESE PAGES: From this main hallway, you can ascend the stairs to a roof-deck that looks over all of Coronado Island and the sea. We found this vintage slate-topped table at Obsolete, in Culver City; the light piece above is Knotty Bubbles by Lindsey Adelman. The rocking chair came from Sonoma; it adds a playfulness that prevents the room from feeling too sparse and contemporary.

OPPOSITE: I found these beautiful 1890 wooden bowls from Belgium at the San Francisco Antiques show, and they set the tone for the whole house before it had even broken ground.
ABOVE: These homeowners are not big cooks, but they wanted the kitchen to feel very open—like it's part of the house. So we kept it spare and neutral, without a lot of ornament.

159

Juxtaposing antiques with modern pieces helps a room feel timeless. Here, we tucked an antique Swedish sideboard from Galerie Half behind the snaking stair, and an English wingback chair beside a sculptural white oak piece. The accordion-like side table at left was from an auto mechanic's shop and was once used to lift cars.

OPPOSITE: For the antique bench, we devised a summer cushion and a winter cushion; the latter is mohair, so you can come in from the heated pool in the winter and not be too cold. ABOVE: The pool house bathroom was very important because he surfs, and often enters right from the beach. The custom towel hamper is wrapped in leather. FOLLOWING PAGES: Pouring into the pool, a gurgling fountain brings an added sense of serenity.

PREVIOUS PAGES: A custom
canopy bed (designed with
the mattress at a higher height
than normal, so the ocean can
be seen from bed) brings
structure to the primary
bedroom. RIGHT: We made the
shelves in the office from a
dark oak, then lacquered
them. The Helene Aumont
table looks a bit like a
sawhorse, but in walnut with a
leather top it's very refined.

HOOK POND

After Gregory and I were married on Hook Pond in East Hampton, where his family has had a six-acre beach compound forever, we fell in love all over again: with a shingle-style colonial that sits proudly on the land. The structure was originally built in 1815 to preside over Main Street, and, in 1923, moved to its current roost near the Maidstone Club. Until recently the house was mostly used for guest spillover, and we decided to take it under our wing and make it our own. It was well worth some TLC: it stands next to a towering old walnut tree and fronts sprawling lawns beside Hook Pond, making it an ideal hideaway for our family during summertime visits with James, who lives to run and run across the grass.

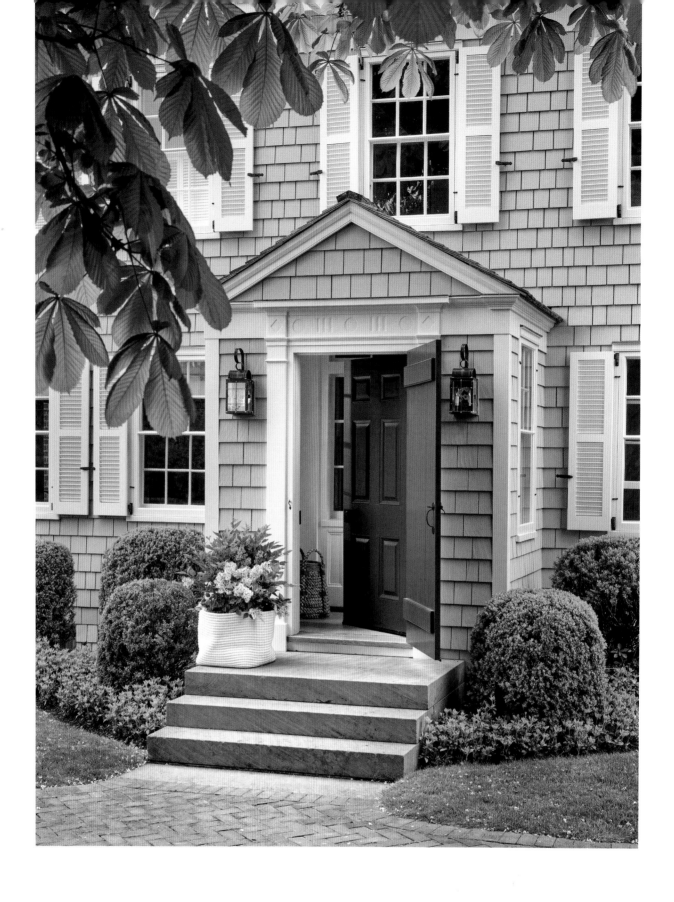

ABOVE: We preserved and repainted the home's original storm door and secondary door, a layered New England classic. OPPOSITE: I brought in sconces I designed; I like the mix of the contemporary in an old-fashioned house. PAGE 174: After nightfall, these letters light up and cast a beautiful reflection in the rooms. PAGE 175: I bought the table in our dining room for my first house in Santa Monica, and I've been lugging it around with me from house to house ever since. I love the finish on it. I found the old secretary at left in the basement, repainted it, and distressed the finish.

The East Hampton community—founded in 1648—tends to value old things over new. Residents share a real appreciation for the type of centuries-old architecture that makes this an iconic summertime retreat. That's something we value, too. So we kept the house's original pine floors intact along with all the rest of its heirloom-quality bones, including the exposed beams overhead. Instead of architectural revisions, this project was an exercise in just how much you can achieve with decor alone. We freshened up the paint here, hung wallpaper there, and curated a stockpile of antiques and custom pieces throughout. Most of my design projects are ground-up construction, so cozying up a house just for us without having to touch the architecture was a true treat.

None of our choices could be too precious.

It's the beach, after all, and I wanted to bring a relaxed note of Southern California to the house. Days are spent walking on the sand; kayaking and paddleboarding the pond; splaying out on grassy waterside knolls; and perfecting our tennis game. A casual, simple feeling was paramount. Gregory and I pillaged the house's attic for old furniture he loved from his childhood, and poked about in local antique shops for treasure that could be refinished with a cleaner twist. Because there's no better place to gauge an item's durability than the beach, the house also became a de facto design laboratory for my burgeoning furniture and fabric collections.

PREVIOUS PAGES: This rug kicked off my collection for The Rug Company: I asked them for blue rugs and this was the only one they had. The ship captain's chair is a circa 1900s Italian antique. OPPOSITE: My tête-à-tête for A. Rudin found an idyllic perch on the slate floors of the sunroom overlooking Hook Pond. This room is double aspect, overlooking the pond on one side and the lawn and gardens on the other.

It was important to us to delineate the home from other structures on the property, so while it has a very East Coast formality, it also has an edge: quirky and sexy. We installed custom grass-cloth wallpaper of my own design, which added even more character to the rooms, and incorporated such disparate pieces as a Georgian-era leather and wood antique chair, an early 1900s mahogany canopy bed we spotted in the attic and repainted, and a custom industrial metal EAST sign that illuminates the breakfast nook. Fortuitously, my collection for The Rug Company stemmed from this house. I'd been hunting hard for blue rugs and could only find one to choose from amid their many offerings, so

ABOVE: I found my fish plates in the gift shop at the phenomenal Monterey Bay Aquarium. OPPOSITE: In our small breakfast room off the kitchen, I brought in my emerald sofa for A. Rudin and rug from The Rug Company. FOLLOWING PAGES: One of my favorite things about this kitchen is that it's very small, which makes it cozy. We added the window seats, which peer out onto the swing; the speckled plates are from March in San Francisco. PAGES 184–85: I had my fabrics for Kravet made into outdoor pillows, shown here.

ABOVE: Every side table needs a couple of *objets*, and it's nice if one nods to the locale—like this matchbox from the historic Maidstone Club in East Hampton. OPPOSITE: I found this timeworn bed quilt in the attic; I love it because it's all hand-done. The desk is my own design for Palecek. FOLLOWING PAGES: Our primary bedroom overlooks Hook Pond; the color of the canopy bed echoes the sky at twilight.

I called up and asked, "Why do you only have one blue rug?" Their response was a call to action: "Design us more!"

Although we initially planned this house as a summer getaway, we've found that we love visiting East Hampton in autumn and winter just as much, especially now that we're mostly based in Connecticut. All the throngs of summer have taken their last Jitney out of town, and the village feels blissfully quiet—like our own secret.

ABOVE: Coalie cuddled in pillows made from my own collection for Kravet. OPPOSITE: In our daughter's room, I employed one of my favorite rugs: a woven Serena & Lily carpet that's great for kids because, at about an inch thick, it's so cushioned it's practically a bumper. FOLLOWING PAGES: We spend every afternoon on this dock over the pond, as kayakers drift by. The pillows are from my own collection for Kravet.

DEVIL'S COVE

Tucked away on a glimmering lake cove in Texas, this very sleek, contemporary house was designed by my extremely talented friend the Houston-based architect Michael Landrum. "It sits on a peninsula ringed by these incredible cypress and live oaks," Landrum says. "We wanted the house to be a glass pavilion that was an exercise in stealth. It's really a magical spot."

The homeowners are a couple I met while hiking up the Ute Trail in Aspen years ago. We ended up out until the wee hours of the night dancing at the Caribou Club and have been close ever since.

This is the second house I've designed for them and their three children, and it's their dream home: a stunning, museum-like structure right on the lake where the husband had always wanted to have their primary residence. The locals call this pocket of the lake Devil's Cove. Well, if that's true, then sign me up for hell: the place is a perfect juxtaposition of natural beauty and nearby culture.

Although Landrum and I removed the extremely dated house that formerly stood on the plot and wasn't worth keeping, we tried to echo its monumental feel. "It's sort of a double level site, so it drops pretty dramatically from street level down to water level," Landrum says. He designed the house so that the grandeur of it only reveals itself once you're within the property. "Indelicately put, it's a mullet house," Landrum says. "It's very deceptive. It appears as if it's an extremely modest, small house, but once the gate is opened and you drive up to the parking court and entry pavilion and walk inside, you've got an entry gallery and a grand set of stairs that takes you down to the main level. And it's there that you realize, oh, my gosh, this house completely unfolds as you traverse the steps down. And it's nothing like what you would envision from the street. There's a complete sense of arrival and mystery and surprise, which I think is great. I think it really knocks the socks off people."

The architecture is a fittingly industrial envelope for what's inside, where the family has collected furniture and art that are also a contrast to the setting. You'll see the slogan "Keep Austin Weird" on bumper stickers around town, and this house lives up to it in the best ways, from its concrete tub to the taxidermy bobcat in the study. The home is formal in its voluminous structure, and I love that my clients were not afraid of using color (note

My clients' beautiful Claude Lalanne crocodile bench is a star of the living room, so we placed it center stage. All the sky-high ceilings and floor-to-ceiling windows give the home the effect of a sprawling and airy art museum. The piece above the fireplace is by Katharina Grosse.

ABOVE: The exterior is meant to recede a bit, letting nature take the lead. OPPOSITE: The John Dickinson chairs in the dining space are some of my favorites; he was one of the designers whose work I loved the most in my early days. FOLLOWING PAGES: We designed the whole kitchen around the Carpenters Workshop light fixture. After dark, it casts a transfixing glow on the copper cabinets.

ABOVE: Lake life is about being outside as much as possible. OPPOSITE: Decades-old trees provide abundant shade over the pool that's pure bliss in the height of a Texas summer. FOLLOWING PAGES: Collected art and objects bring a curated impact to the study, while the curved, sculptural sofas by Vladimir Kagan allow a certain languidness and breathing room for juxtaposition.

the parakeet sofas in the living room) and finding the unusual to fill it. One of the clients grew up in an antiques-loving family, and her marching orders were clear: "I don't want one thing from a showroom. I want it all to be interesting and funky. And we don't want it to look like we live in Texas."

The architecture itself is a foil for the art: a Banksy hangs here, a James Turrell there. In the building phase, these clients and I went to Art Basel and searched galleries from Los Angeles to Europe for things that really meant something to them. Not all was new, of course—treasured pieces played key roles. We designed the whole living room around a beautiful Claude Lalanne crocodile bench that also had pride of place in their previous home. Here, we softened it a bit by surrounding it with sculptural sofas my client found. Above the hearth, a piece by German artist Katharina Grosse supplies riveting color; hung above the stair, an oversize painting of cacti by Dallas artist Rosson Crow echoes regional landscapes in an eye-candy way.

Nothing in this home is standard-issue or typical. That includes the kitchen, which we built with copper cabinet fronts. This is a family that loves to cook, as you can tell from the patina on the surfaces. You can see where their hands have touched a drawer and cabinet again and again, and the surface is wearing down slowly over the years. I love that they don't keep it too pristine. They live hard in this house, and it suits them to the core.

PREVIOUS PAGES: A Claude Lalanne gilt bronze chair inspired by the ginkgo leaf is an artful seat in the primary bedroom. The homeowners' bed is a carved Spanish antique; the bench at the foot of the bed is Paul Evans. OPPOSITE: In the primary bathroom, the soaking tub is made of concrete—a fitting finish that mixes beautifully with the wildness of the tree branches beyond the windows.

PREVIOUS PAGES: The stone coffee table in the family room may never be moved, it's so heavy! I love the clawfoot table from Blackman Cruz under the James Turrell painting; the piece above the fire is by Banksy. ABOVE: A large-scale painting by Texas artist Rosson Crow brings a beautiful jolt of color to this stair hall. OPPOSITE: A black plaster ceiling supplies shimmer overhead in the wine room.

212

LAKE LAGUNITAS

Marin County is pure enchantment: a treasure trove of emerald shores and exultant gardens. In this part of the world, the landscapes grow thick and lush; new plants appear to sprout from the earth, fully formed, seemingly overnight. Our goal for my young clients' new farmhouse—a gabled beauty designed with the help of architects Ken Linsteadt and Molly Nolan Layshock—was pure Marin with its craftsman detailing, but combined with an East Coast Hamptons vibe that will always feel timeless. (Note the new—yet already deliciously overgrown—wisteria that scuttles up the porch columns. Indeed, this is such fertile land that in years past, there was a nursery on my clients' property; in this area everything grows like a weed!)

The house sits on a hilly plot overlooking the nearby town. We were determined to keep the beautiful sea of pine trees that have stood watch over the land for decades. But for the rest of the house, we leaned as fresh as the salty marine layer drifting in off the bay. A light and airy feeling was a must, along with plenty of defined, private areas for members of this family of five to retreat

to for quiet moments. To lend the interior a centuries-old feeling, we built a massive stone core with a fireplace in the center of the house. It acts as an anchor to the surrounding formal areas, creates more intimate spaces, and prevents the great room from reading too massive. It even has a secret: the bookshelves built within it are on a hinge and slowly glide open to reveal the entry closet. I also love the primary bathroom's abundant skylights, which give you the feeling that you're bathing in an actual tree house—a feeling further enhanced by an indoor/outdoor shower with a glass atrium ceiling and doors that open to the terrace.

PREVIOUS PAGES AND ABOVE: A Munder Skiles bench and a duo of matching planters bring added elegance to the approach. We painted a lot of the exterior decks, which was fun; you don't see that often in new construction, and it adds a lot of charm. OPPOSITE: The Lucca Antiques chandelier and antique secretary from Country House in Montecito were our starting points for the living room. I love an antique rug; this one anchors the sitting area beautifully.

The kitchen is a testament to this lovely couple's hospitality, with a hulking island and custom walnut chopping board for her (the family's chef de cuisine), as well as a sliding marble backsplash behind the range that opens to reveal gadgets and a stash of spices tucked within the wall itself. And because he finds washing and drying dishes therapeutic—and it is, especially when using his preferred linen towels—we built a separate dishwashing station that features an industrial stainless steel sink and French doors that fling open to a pea-gravel pathway into the garden. He deems the area his sanctuary.

Speaking of sanctuaries: we constructed an octagonal dining room just off the main living space that's stained a deep juniper green. Because it's so formal, and a bit of a shuffle from the kitchen (it's accessed through the butler's pantry), I knew they wouldn't use it often with their three kids. That gave me carte blanche to transform it into a dining room that doubles as a library. It differs visually from the rest of the home. Where most spaces feel very light, open, and airy, this room is stoic, dark, and sexy, with a walnut table that transforms into a poker table. Shelves chockablock with books lent an instant solidity to the room. When you close the pocket doors, it's like you've entered a portal to the past, perhaps an old Manhattan library's reading room. What better place to grab a dram of whiskey and a book and watch the fog roll in?

OPPOSITE: In the octagonal dining space, we installed a Richard Wrightman table that echoes the zinc ceiling. The latter was the starting inspiration for my forthcoming lighting collection with Visual Comfort. FOLLOWING PAGES: I don't do two matching sofas very often, but I thought it was needed in this house; these, by John Saladino, have a beautiful envelope. The coffee table is my own design.

OPPOSITE: These two are wonderful cooks, and we had endless meetings about the kitchen, which were worth it. ABOVE: The husband adores doing dishes, so we built him a dishwashing station with stainless steel finishes and a pair of dishwashers at the ready. He's out of the way of the rest of the kitchen and has the best view in the house, overlooking the gardens.

ABOVE: The indoor/outdoor shower with a double showerhead in the primary suite makes you feel like you're floating in the treetops, thanks to an atrium ceiling that peeps out on the neighboring pine trees. OPPOSITE: A light-filled pass-through.

FOUR TREES

With James growing up in a blink, Gregory and I had a realization. It was time to put down roots in our dream house near Gregory's family on the East Coast—the one that would check all our boxes. We needed to create the perfect backdrop for our family to evolve.

It seemed like an impossible ask. The list of things we had to have would strike fear into even the most capable realtor's heart! We longed for a home with a garden that would feel substantial to us and our growing family, and that would echo the manor houses I fell in love with in the English countryside and studied in design school. Gregory hoped for something that would be reminiscent of the Chestnut Hill house where he grew up. Good schools were essential, and sophisticated restaurants nearby equally so. Along with all that, proximity to an international airport was key. James is already a card-carrying member of the globetrotting glitterati—emphasis on glitter.

Enter Greenwich, Connecticut, a town that has always been equal parts gracious and genteel. On a weekend trip to visit family on the East Coast, we

stumbled upon this 1928 house designed by Edwin Sherrill Dodge and knew it was The One. Who would have thought someone would tear me away from the beach? But finally, I could decorate in the way in which I was trained in London. With its brick facade and neo-Georgian massing, it reminded me of an English boarding school—our own little echo of Eton College.

We moved in just as I was turning sixty, and what a perfect birthday gift to have my beautiful family living in the kind of house I'd always dreamed of! (Later, I learned that one of my longtime girl crushes, Mary Tyler Moore, had a neighboring house—so the home was in great company.)

We didn't know it when we bought the Georgian country house, but the home has a vibrant history. Featured in *House & Garden* and *Town & Country* magazines in its day, Four Trees (named, presumably, for the quartet of trees flanking its entrance facade) was designed as a country house for the prominent Truesdale family of Park Avenue. It originally presided over sixty acres, with gardens designed by Ellen Biddle Shipman—one of the earliest female landscape architects. Those gardens were overgrown and junglelike by the time we got to them, so we spent months working to bring them back to their manicured and tidy 1920s-era aesthetic. Our goal was to revive the Shipman-instilled grandeur.

Design legends Billy Baldwin and Ruby Ross Wood had early hands in decorating the house over the years, but time had not been kind. The architectural charm was still

OPPOSITE: The sunroom in our 1928 Greenwich, Connecticut, home presides over the four-acre garden where we live snow or shine; I adore the original stone floor that was once an exterior terrace. The chair in the back corner is my Malawi chair that I designed for Palecek; we found the red chairs in England, and had them painted white and upholstered in Holland & Sherry fabric. I designed the bench at right for the room, and upholstered it in Sandra Jordan alpaca. FOLLOWING PAGES: Our lower garden, which we stocked with McKinnon and Harris garden furniture and boxwoods to accompany the existing boxwood trim designed by legendary landscape architect Ellen Biddle Shipman.

there, including an original curved staircase—but other choices, like the wallpapers hung in every room, were just not to my taste. I felt it was my job to bring back the gravitas and magnetism the house once had.

I always think that in designing a home, one should start with an object that they love and try to build the house around it, not the other way around. I kicked off the palette of the living spaces with a new rug I designed for The Rug Company, bringing muted tones up the walls in a brilliant gloss that would bounce daylight around the rooms like a mirror. On our travels, Gregory and I found another unlikely muse, a 1910 oil painting of the

ABOVE: The lines of this rug bring some lovely movement to the living room. OPPOSITE: This old stone library table from France was the first piece I found for the house, and it's so heavy that it took seven men to bring it through the front door. We kept the colors simple to echo the staircase originally designed by Billy Baldwin; the art piece is by Montauk artist Balcomb Greene. The bench is my own design, a modified and modern take on the English spindle. FOLLOWING PAGES: We created a custom Scandinavian gray-blue for the living room, and it gleams on the home's original Dutch doors and woodwork.

Provincetown Pier by abstract artist Irene Rice Pereira. The misty wharf is done in inky blues, with a red boathouse that serves as a punctuation point.

I completely gutted the kitchen to make what is now one large cook space and a bar done with cupboards by Plain English of Britain. Throughout, I used Fine Paints of Europe colors, whose richly pigmented tones and high gloss finish saved me. I was concerned that I would get depressed living in a very different light than what I'd been used to in Montecito, so I decided to keep the house very light and airy and refrained from going too muddy or too tonal with the color. The result is quite bouncy and bright. I kept the window coverings spare and clean, too, to allow in as much sunlight as possible. There's not a lot of ornament on the walls because I wanted to hold true to myself and my minimalist California roots.

The dining room is one of my favorite rooms ever for entertaining. The existing hand-painted de Gournay wallcovering that depicts North American river views makes every walk into the room feel like a barefoot stroll in a pastoral scene. To do it justice, I added a seventeen-foot-long French pine table paired with wonderfully beat-up green leather English Chippendale chairs. Altogether, it gives the full effect of arriving in the country. The perfect place for an evening, and a family tree, to flourish and unfold.

PREVIOUS PAGES: Integrated nickel drawer pulls built into the Plain English cabinets give the room a modern touch, so it doesn't look overly traditional. OPPOSITE: James is the ruling queen of our kitchen, which I designed to feel like an old English larder. I bought the lantern over the island the same day we closed on the house and completely restored it, adding rope for texture.

OPPOSITE: A round bench brings more seating to a bistro table than you might ever have thought possible. ABOVE: We transformed the home's de facto speakeasy—a former hidden alcohol storage space—into a morning wet bar just off our breakfast room for coffee, painting it and all the original moldings a custom blue by Fine Paints of Europe that echoes the vintage Swiss light.

PREVIOUS PAGES: Our primary bedroom suite is enormous—probably the largest we've ever had at 1,500 square feet—so I cozied it up with Schumacher by Colette Cosentino wallpaper. To give it the feel of an English country house, we brought in a Jamb sofa from London in mustard linen and an alpaca rug from Marc Phillips. OPPOSITE: There's nothing like an armchair by the fire. ABOVE: I numbered the cupboard doors on our Plain English closet because Gregory is always absconding with my closet space! I'm a huge proponent of closed doors; I just don't love the exposed look of open closets.

170

EXTERIOR SIDING

on, so that if a slight variation in the
lapping is necessary, it can be distrib-
uted among several pieces rather than
taken up by just one or two. It is also
a good idea to mark the location of each
piece of siding on the corner boards and
at some other internal points to
so that you will know exactly where
each piece is to go; in addition, you can
string a line between these points to
make sure that each piece is horizontal.
   For best results, siding should be
fairly well seasoned. The siding should
be applied during dry weather and
should never go on when wet or over
wet sheathing.

Bevel Siding

   The first step in applying b
ing after the corner b
to tack a strip of
bottom of

**Fig. A. Bevel siding joined at the corners
with a mitered joint.**

so that it can be fitted around these
openings. See Figs. 6 and 7. In view
of this, it would be wise to figure out
the spacing of the siding before it goes

The siding should be cut with a nice
even joint and you want to have each
piece fitting rather snugly against the
adjoining pieces and the corner boards.
In very high class work, a diagonal
cut is used where one piece of siding
joins the next.
   Siding nailed over wood sheathing
can be rust-resisting with 8d nails. These must
be driven about every 16". The nails
are spaced about every 16". These must
piece so that every overl
two nails at each
the siding at each

EXTERIOR SIDING

177

CAN'T LIVE WITHOUT

1818 Collective
the1818collective.com

The Antique and Artisan Gallery
theantiqueandartisangallery.com

Blackman Cruz
blackmancruz.com

Carpenters Workshop Gallery
carpentersworkshopgallery.com

Casa Gusto
getthegusto.com

Charles Edwards
charlesedwards.com

Counter-Space
counter-space.com

Country House Antiques
countryhouseantiques.com

Coup D'Etat
coupdetatsf.com

Cove Landing NYC
@covelanding

The Flat
theflatwestport.com

Frances Palmer Pottery
francespalmerpottery.com

Galerie Half
galeriehalf.com

Galerie Provenance
galerieprovenance.com

Guinevere
guinevere.co.uk

Howe London
howelondon.com

Jamb
jamb.co.uk

JED Interior Design and Antiques
jeddesign.com

JF Chen
jfchen.com

John Bird Antiques
johnbirdantiques.com

Kravet
kravet.com

La Tuile à Loup
latuilealoup.com

Lee Stanton
leestanton.com

Lief
liefgallery.com

Lindsey Adelman Studio
lindseyadelman.com

Lucca Antiques
luccaantiques.com

March
marchsf.com

Mitchell Denburg Collection
mitchelldenburg.com

Monc XIII
monc13.com

Munder Skiles
munder-skiles.com

Nickey Kehoe
nickeykehoe.com

Obsolete
obsoleteinc.com

Palecek
palecek.com

Pat McGann
patmcganngallery.com

Paul Ferrante
paulferrante.com

Plain English
plainenglishdesign.com

Plain Goods
plain-goods.com

Richard Wrightman
richardwrightman.com

Robert Kime
robertkime.com

Rose Tarlow
rosetarlow.com

Rose Uniacke
roseuniacke.com

The Rug Company
therugcompany.com

Saladino
saladinostyle.com

Sawkille Co.
sawkille.com

Sigmar
sigmarlondon.com

Soane Britain
soane.co.uk

The Urban Electric Co.
urbanelectric.com

The Well
@thewellsummerland

Westenholz Antiques &
Interior Decoration
westenholz.co.uk

William Laman Furniture.Garden.
Antiques
williamlaman.com

Wyeth
wyeth.nyc

ACKNOWLEDGMENTS

Firstly, I would like to thank my bathtub and the Loire Valley—the region of France that produces Sancerre wine, which I consumed often while trying to put this book together.

To my loyal clients who trusted the process and allowed me to guide them in building the safe harbor that they can call home—thank you, I could never have done this without you. I am so thankful for this gift I have been given: to be able to work for now celebrating thirty years in this fascinating profession and all I've seen and learned along the way.

To team JAM and all who have passed through it for keeping moving forward, and the book team, including Jill Cohen, for putting wheels in motion; Monsieur Trevor Tondro, who started this journey with me in Montecito and traveled far and wide to get the right shots; designers Doug Turshen and Steve Turner for teaching me what a high resolution image was and placing it so perfectly on the page; writer Kathryn O'Shea-Evans for listening so intently and helping make sense of all the ideas in my head; and editor Kathleen Jayes for remaining calm and carrying on throughout.

Thank you to John Saladino: you were my true design inspiration from the first day of design school.

Thank you to all of the Paleceks and Kravets for whom I have designed successful worldwide furniture and fabric collections. You are like my second family.

To The Rug Company, who trusted my designs from the get-go and produced them so magnificently for many rooms in this book.

Thank you to Robert O'Block, who has supported us unconditionally in all of our crazy adventures, and to Christine Kennedy for your wisdom along the way.

Thank you to all the artisans who have worked so closely with us to create these beautiful spaces with their exceptional skills.

To my mother and father, who followed all my endeavors with great joy: I so wish you could still be here to see these pages.

To my darling late Coalie: from sea-to-sea lounging on the floor, my friend, you were the best accessory.

And finally, my deepest gratitude to my husband, Gregory, and our daughter, James. Thank you for always being there with your immense love and support, making me laugh, and creating our beautiful life . . . while also managing to hand me that glass of wine in the bathtub at the end of the day. This is all for you.

PHOTOGRAPHY CREDITS:

Neil Landino: Front cover, 229, 231, 232–33, 234, 236–37, 240, 241, 242–43, 245, 246, 247, 250

Sara Prince: 2–3, 44

Trevor Tondro: 5, 6, 11, 16, 18, 19, 20–21, 22–23, 24, 25, 26–27, 28–29, 30, 31, 32–33, 34–35, 36, 37, 38, 39, 40–41, 42, 43, 45, 46, 47, 48–49, 51, 52–53, 54–55, 56, 58, 59, 60–61, 62, 63, 64, 65, 66, 67, 68, 69, 71, 95, 96–97, 98, 99, 101, 102–3, 104, 105, 106–7, 108, 109, 110–11, 114, 115, 117, 119, 120, 121, 122, 124, 125, 126–27, 129, 131, 132, 133, 135, 136, 137, 138–39, 140, 141, 142–43, 172, 173, 174, 176–77, 179, 180, 181, 186, 187, 188–89, 196, 199, 200–201, 202, 203, 204–5, 206–7, 208, 210–11, 212, 213, 235, 238–39, 248–49, 251, 252, 255, back cover

Roger Davies: 8, 147, 148–49, 150, 152–53, 154–55, 156–57, 158, 159, 160–61, 162, 163, 164–65, 166–67, 168–69

Tess Albrecht: 13

Brandon Huttenlocher: 15, 113, 123, 195, 215

William Abranowicz: 72, 74–75, 76, 77, 79, 80–81, 82–83, 84, 86, 87, 88, 89, 90, 91

Getty/Mauricio Paiz: 93

Getty/Cavan Images: 145

Arianna Tettamanzi: 171, 175, 182–83, 184–85, 190, 191, 192–93

Lisa Petrole: 198

Paul Dyer: 216–17, 218, 225, 226, 227

José Manuel Aldora: 219, 221, 222–23, 224

Lisa Miller Design for The Rug Company: Endpapers

First published in the United States of America in 2025 by Rizzoli International Publications, Inc.
49 West 27th Street
New York, NY 10001
www.rizzoliusa.com

Copyright © 2024 Jeffrey Alan Marks
Text: Kathryn O'Shea-Evans
Foreword: John Saladino

Art Credits:
Page 52 and reverse of back ends: George Condo, Artwork in situ © 2024 George Condo / Artists Rights Society (ARS), New York

Page 196: Claude Lalanne, 'Crocodile' Bench, 2015 © 2024 Artists Rights Society (ARS), New York / ADAGP, Paris
Katharina Grosse, Untitled, 2016 © 2024 Artists Rights Society (ARS), New York / VG Bild-Kunst, Bonn

Publisher: Charles Miers
Senior Editor: Kathleen Jayes
Design: Doug Turshen with Steve Turner
Production Manager: Colin Hough-Trapp
Managing Editor: Lynn Scrabis

Printed in Hong Kong

2025 2026 2027 2028 / 10 9 8 7 6 5 4 3 2 1

ISBN: 978-0-8478-4515-6

Library of Congress Control Number: 2024945767

Visit us online:
Instagram.com/RizzoliBooks
Facebook.com/RizzoliNewYork
X: @Rizzoli_Books
Youtube.com/user/RizzoliNY

FSC
MIX
Paper | Supporting responsible forestry
FSC™ C023053
www.fsc.org